Please visit our website, www.garethstevens.com. For a free color catalog of all our high-quality books, call toll free 1-800-542-2595 or fax 1-877-542-2596.

Library of Congress Cataloging-in-Publication Data

Griffin, Ingrid.
The story of Cassiopeia / by Ingrid Griffin.
p. cm. — (Stories in the stars)
Includes index.
ISBN 978-1-4824-2661-8 (pbk.)
ISBN 978-1-4824-2662-5 (6 pack)
ISBN 978-1-4824-2663-2 (library binding)
1. Stars — Juvenile literature. 2. Cassiopeia (Constellation) — Juvenile literature. 3. Mythology, Roman — Juvenile literature. I. Title.
QB801.7 G75 2016
398.20937—d23

Published in 2016 by
Gareth Stevens Publishing
111 East 14th Street, Suite 349
New York, NY 10003

Copyright © 2016 Gareth Stevens Publishing

Designer: Nicholas Domiano
Editor: Therese Shea

Photo credits: Cover, p. 1 (constellation) Dorling Kindersley/Getty Images; cover, p. 1 (space) ECKHARD SLAWIK/Science Library Photo/Getty Images; pp. 3–24 (interior texture) USBFCO/Shutterstock.com; p. 5 angelinast/Shutterstock.com; p. 7 Anders Peter Photography/Shutterstock.com; p. 9 Buyenlarge/Archive Photos/Getty Images; p. 11 Library of Congress/Wikimedia Commons; p. 13 Print Collector/Hulton Archive/Getty Images; p. 15 © iStockphoto.com/ZU_09; p. 17 Kean Collection/Getty Images; p. 19 Heritage Images/Hulton Fine Art Collection/Getty Images; p. 21 Dorling Kindersley/Getty Images.

Printed in the United States of America

CPSIA compliance information: Batch #CS15GS: For further information contact Gareth Stevens, New York, New York at 1-800-542-2595.

CONTENTS

Boldface words appear in the glossary.

A Queen in the Sky

A constellation is a group of stars that forms a shape. Cassiopeia (kas-ee-oh-PEE-ah) is one constellation. Five bright stars form a "w" in the night sky. The constellation is named for Cassiopeia, a woman from Greek **myths**.

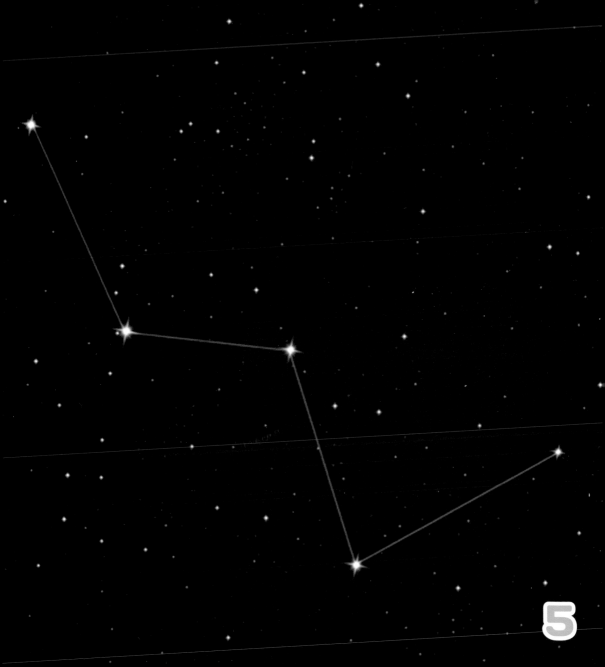

A Mistake

Cassiopeia was married to King Cepheus (SEE-fee-uhs). She told people she was more beautiful than the lovely sea **nymphs** called Nereids (NIH-ree-uhdz). The Nereids were angered by this. They asked the god of the sea, Poseidon, to **punish** Cassiopeia.

Poseidon

7

The Sea Monster

Poseidon sent a sea monster called Cetus (SEE-tuhs) to ruin Cepheus's kingdom. Some say Cetus was a serpent, or snake. Others say it was a whale. Cetus is also a constellation found near the constellations Cassiopeia and Cepheus.

A Sacrifice

Cetus did great harm to King Cepheus's land. Cepheus wanted to help his people. He asked an **oracle** what he could do. The oracle said Cepheus had to **sacrifice** his beautiful daughter Andromeda (an-DRAH-muh-duh) to the sea monster.

Queen Cassiopeia and King Cepheus didn't want to lose their daughter. However, they didn't know what else to do. They chained her to a rock so that Cetus the sea monster could kill her. Andromeda was in great danger.

13

Perseus Appears

Then, a young hero named Perseus (PUHR-see-uhs) appeared in the sky above. He had winged **sandals** that made him fly. He saw the beautiful woman below chained to a rock. Perseus fell in love with Andromeda at once.

15

Perseus promised he would save Andromeda if she married him. She said yes. Just then, Cetus appeared. After a terrible battle, brave Perseus killed the sea monster. He then freed Andromeda and returned her to her family.

17

At the wedding of Perseus and Andromeda, her uncle Phineus (FIN-ee-uhs) said he himself should be the one to marry the princess. Perseus used the head of a monster named Medusa to turn Phineus to stone. However, Cassiopeia and Cepheus turned to stone, too.

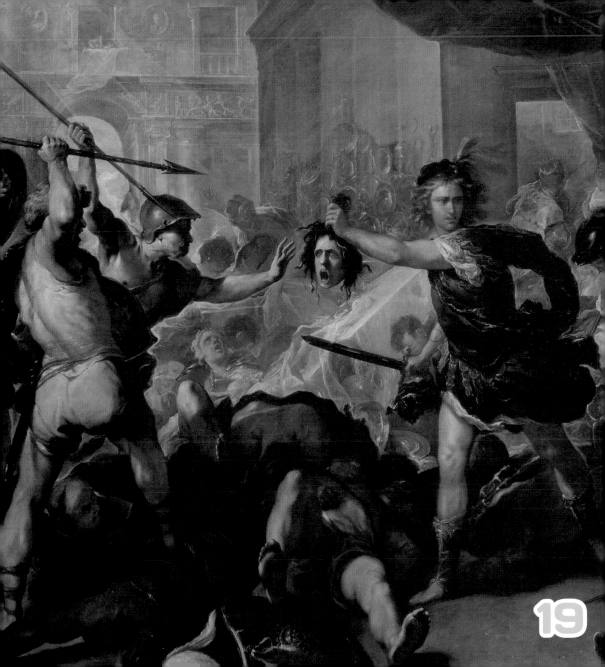

19

A Final Punishment

Poseidon placed Cassiopeia in the sky. As punishment for her **vanity**, she spends half the year upside down. Cassiopeia is usually pictured on her **throne**. Try to find her next time you're watching the night sky. Look for the "w"!

21

GLOSSARY

myth: a story that was told by an ancient people to explain something

nymph: in stories, a spirit that lives in nature in the shape of a young woman

oracle: in ancient Greece, a person through whom a god was believed to speak

punish: to make someone suffer for a crime or bad behavior

sacrifice: to kill a person or animal as an offering to please a god

sandal: a light, open shoe with straps worn during warm weather

throne: the special chair for a king, queen, or other powerful person

vanity: the quality of people who have too much pride in their own appearance or abilities

FOR MORE INFORMATION

BOOKS

McCaughrean, Geraldine. *Perseus*. Chicago, IL: Carus Publishing, 2005.

Owings, Lisa. *The Constellation Cassiopeia: The Story of the Queen*. Mankato, MN: Child's World, 2013.

Troupe, Thomas Kingsley. *The Story of Cassiopeia: A Roman Constellation Myth*. North Mankato, MN: Picture Window Books, 2013.

WEBSITES

Astronomy for Kids
www.kidsastronomy.com/astroskymap/constellation_hunt.htm
Play a game to learn how to spot constellations.

Greek Mythology for Kids
greece.mrdonn.org/myths.html
Find many links to the most famous stories of Greek mythology.

INDEX